PETIT MORTS

Meditations on Love and Death

poems by

Mukund Gnanadesikan

Finishing Line Press
Georgetown, Kentucky

PETIT MORTS

Meditations on Love and Death

ACKNOWLEDGMENTS

Ayaskala (To A Grieving Mother)
Bluepepper (Parasites)
Datura (Before You Walk Away, Trigger Warning)
Flumes (In Memoriam. Life Ends in Immolation)
Ginosko (A Conversation, View from a Hospital Window)
Livina Review (In the ICU)
Poesis (A Bullet's Tale, Under My Skin)
Poetic Sun (On the Road to Pololu)
Remington Review (Lepidoptera)
Sledgehammer Lit (Chanteuse)
Stardust Review (Exhortation, A Love Matured)

Publisher: Leah Huete de Maines
Editor: Christen Kincaid
Cover Art: Dominik Gnanadesikan
Author Photo: Art & Clarity Photography, Napa, CA
Cover Design: Elizabeth Maines McCleavy

Order online: www.finishinglinepress.com
also available on amazon.com

Author inquiries and mail orders:
Finishing Line Press
PO Box 1626
Georgetown, Kentucky 40324
USA

Table of Contents

View From a Hospital Window

The monitor beeps. A buttercup sun
dispenses blessings through reticulated filter
of mournful fenestrated clouds.

Beyond glass, I see the swaying beach grass,
threatening to flee the dunes and tumble
seaward, where adventure beckons in a maroon skiff.

Sing to me again,
"Amazing Grace."
In your delicate soprano,

I hear a quiver of unshed tears.
I cannot sate your hunger, unsatisfied
by sympathy's insubstantial appetizer.

Pour for me a Dixie cup of water.
Do not let the curtain close.
The world grows dark.

Wander With Me

The route is undetermined.
Join me, link fingers
Hands are made
to grasp and hold,
though mine prove fallible
allow too much to fall away.
What should be embraced

escapes and shatters,
colliding with unrepentant asphalt.
Check your hesitation, your mistrust.
I will hang them in the closet;
You may collect them later.
For now, in mutual embrace
skin to skin, we share a dream.

To A Newly Grieving Mother

I would feel with you
Share each constricted breath
Loosen you from ligature of pain
If only it were possible.

Tragedy's frangible shell
Cracks into curved white shards,
Begs for repair, but I
Lacking knowledge, impotently hold you.

The serpent grief injects her venom,
Paralytic to all breath of hope.
So urgent the need for antidote
To despair's slow-darkening vision

Tears spent like silver dollars
Waste not in my eyes.
Though I cry silently
Here I am, together scars grow fainter.

Erokinesis

Yellow flame tickles
the smooth glass beaker,

Its contents rise, slow-dance in close quarters.
Heat unlocks potential,

prods molecules to move,
grind one another.

Frictional transactions
fuel froth, vaporous release.

A switch turns off:
devoid of fire, all is quiescent.

The night gives alms
for chemical expenditures.

Nightmare in Retrograde

The quilt covers you, almond eyes shut, blue lips unmoving.
Lines are disconnected, the surgeon stares at a sterile floor.
The nurse brushes her hair, washes it, makes it straight.

"Let her go," the cruelest mercy ever given;
The doctors point to the pulse ox, wave their white flags, say "We're losing."
Frantic arms pump, pray for new breath, fragile ribs jump like a puppet's arms

"We'll have to stabilize her. The intracranial pressure is too much."
Children's Hospital, a stabbing ringtone: "Knock, Knock, Knocking on Heaven's Door"
We pack, spare clothes, our consciences wax-coated, lungs leaden with foreboding.

"There's still hope," I say. I speak only of open eyes.
The Med-Evac can't carry family, no comfort to the sky-borne.
"We need to get her to Oakland. We don't have the experts here.

Why does her small chest resign itself to silence? Fight, baby girl. You know how.
They say she cannot draw consistent breath; they strip her, shove a tube in, brutal sustenance.
We plead emergent injustice: she was fine and then she wasn't, now she is limp.

Rush to ER, tears drop inside, no time to let them fall upon the ground.
"Mom, I love you." A mother's heart reciprocates self-evident expression.
The headache worsens, she vomits. The gaping mouth of the hourglass runs faster.

Mom, I don't feel good. My head . . .please don't touch me. Just sit here."
The boys down the street go home, it's time for quiet reading
A post-prandial interlude of soccer and frivolity.

You rise and choose half a dozen gourds, map their decorations,
The sun-drenched atmosphere envelops you:
Arrived at the pumpkin patch, lie upon a hay bale, seraphic spread wide.

When We Are Tangled

I have no wish to disassemble our construction.
Too many days I've been a solitary thread,
a life unraveled, doubting the worth of my own fabric;
what purpose could there be for lying motionless, alone?
But years entwine our lives, braid them tightly.
Now indistinct, your earth is mine.
Our roots drink from disparate springs
but common thirst is mutually endured.
And in the night the honeydew of succor
we savor, gifted with affection's common tongue.

Lepidoptera

The white butterfly:
Unadulterated by color or design
Flutters close beside
Its motions nonlinear
As your feet skipping in my mind
Across the blackened pavement.

You are here, reflected in her body,
Alighting on the rosemary
Then there, hiding in oleander
Dipping out of sight
Echoes of wing beats evoke your laughter
Wind awakens memory of citrus on your skin.

She flies away, your opalescent eyes have shut
Must all companions leave?
Beloved child, stay just a moment longer.

A Love Matured

The glowing veil of youth has melted.
Wiped clean, our skins show furrows,
souvenirs of carefree sunlit days.
Honesty wears no enhancements:
years have passed, sometimes in darkness,
and now our fingers know familiar courses
of bodies naked and uneven.
Hands and lips drive blindly with full confidence.
Rhythmic sound of hushed breaths
Drawn in the quiet night,
like susurrus in cornfields.
Untamed, our growing forest:
vines interlocking
roots planted, we are each other's canopy.

Parasites

The Purple Emperor and Zebra Longwing
cannot survive alone on sweetness.

In death comes opportunity.
Decay and bitterness provide satiety.

No charity exists in *Charax*
whose serrated wings will kill a rival.

And am I different?
Watching, feet planted atop absent ancestors

I am no more than a saprophyte
feeding on society's wet stumps,

not allowing second thoughts.
Knowing doubts are lethal to the heartbeat,

we sup upon the corpse that offers, silently,
alms to the open-handed.

I Do Not Exist

until you point ruby red nails.
Sharp fingertips signal recognition,
a bouncing chin nods acknowledgement.
Eyes of a shifting hue have seen me,

comprehended re-animated flesh.
Human once again, I breathe,
color rises to my skin.
I feel my legs, churn them against accursed winds.

Approaching you, I reach for benediction's fingers
seeking fertility of spirit.
I beg you, mortal gods: anoint me.
Suspend the daily shuttering of open windows.

On the Road to Pololu

The newborn piglet stands,
snuffling unmoving mother,
her blood-encrusted body motionless,
closed eyes covered in flies.

A shake of his head begs her
to breathe again, just as she did before.
I fancy that he screams,
curses porcine gods or demons.

What now for the runt?
In dirt he wanders
pacing in circles,
under palms and banyans.

His legacy, like orphans of all species,
no more than a half-torn page,
crimson stained,
final sentence half-effaced.

Speaking in Tongues

Your accent says you do not speak my language—
a barrier we never dare cross.

Who defines these borders, tells us not to cross?
Only fear's shadowy warning signs.

The timbre of your tongue is strange, a sure sign
you do not hail from these parts, neighbors.

And here we are, eyes skeptical of neighbors
who fly above aural perception.

If shoes were switched, I would fear your perception.
Truth's needle stings my besmirched conscience.

When I say, "Welcome", the voice is my conscience
Attempting to put your mind at ease.

You may pass months in restless, lonely slumber.
Hold my hand. I will learn your language.

Passings

Father Time's anaconda
wraps his lazy coils around us.
Such sweet constriction:
we know not what awaits us
when consciousness will let its light be snuffed.

Why spend precious breath
amassing trinkets
in a sullen chest that survives us?
And yet we bleed and sweat for lust,
slaves to shiny coins and throaty carriages.

Daylight's metronome
taps its incessant rhythm
but in a heart's last beat
there is no more possession.
No pearls flicker between our lips.

A Conversation

Reverberations of an empty throat
Carry on the wind wishing to be heard.

    Who says innocents should not be heard?
    So treacherous the shoals of cosmic justice.

Children meet me at the court of cosmic justice.
A thousand wraiths that grasp at sweetest nectar.

    I gorge myself upon the sweetest nectar
    That sits upon your lips awaiting orders.

Soldiers never smile awaiting orders,
Denying evil deeds with thoughts and prayers.

    Of what use are hollow thoughts and prayers
    Under absent God's arches and keystones?

Make light my arches and my keystones,
With your sweet waters fill my hollow throat.

Trigger Warning

The dream is now familiar,
a black and white companion.

No ghosts or goblins are required,
only closed, immobile eyelids.

The repeated image rises:
my naked head, shaven,

chrome gun barrel
resplendent at my temple.

Whose hand holds this instrument?
Unknown and immaterial—

Instants later reddish-purple pool
surrounds my crumpled body.

The white dog lingers,
whimpers,

licks an ear,
sits Shiva by the waning sun.

Sonogram

Who would suspect
The shrimp shaped silhouette,

Clinging avidly to life and safety,
would occasion rainbow flowers,

tears of joy and sadness,
sleep-starved nights

and days of playful frolic?
Your convex forehead concealed

truth and vitality,
monsoon rains and lightning.

When ebon evening wanes
and nimbus skies are cleared

I recall your fragile promise
laid flat, now in full blossom.

Sunday Morning

The leaning tower of hotcakes
stands untouched, awaiting her.

A crow's caw goes unanswered,
reminding me that she will not be coming

down the walnut staircase.
The mornings have been quiet for a year;

no words articulate the hollowness of silence.
The teapot whistles—

hot water is ready, full wakefulness approaches
and we must nourish what is left

upon our bones, well knowing what is missing,
the joyful noise of youth has closed her eyes.

Tell Me Who I Am

To be seen is to be real.
Otherwise, I am intangible,
indistinct from ghosts,
 unicorns and dragons.

Physics and metaphysics
stroll nature's path together,
hands unconsciously entwined.
Venturing into the beyond,

acknowledgment of being
seems simple enough
yet constantly I crave
its sweet colostrum,

significance of which is indeterminate
until defined by you,
your tender words
your beneficent fingers on my cheek.

Exhortation

Arise
unto the soft caress
of solar fingertips.

Imploring eyelids open.
Through the dusty window
morning optimism flows.

Place feet upon the floor.
Gaze hungrily, ingest the yellow-hazed horizon,
no longer paralyzed by fear's curare.

So many bygone days have wasted
staring skyward open-mouthed,
stationary.

Today your spirit rises.
Venture toward me, trust my hands as once you did
when first your veil was lifted.

In Memoriam

The forest of lodgepole pine
cups its massive palms around
this sapphire lake
tonsured in emerald green.
I see the lily pads
where smug-faced frogs
inflate their cheeks at gangly humans
and when the mist falls
we walk, huddled, unprepared
for the chill of rain.
Precipitation sends a cold reminder
of absence with each droplet
that ruffles glassy surface
drowning noise of wind,
of birds,
of peaceful thoughts.
Floating to the surface, memories:
the image of her dead-fish carcass
our exalted gift of life and breath,
shared benediction, confiscated,
laid to rest.
She should be here, skipping through meadows,
and if she were this mist
would taste of rose and sandalwood.
Instead, I choke on bitter almond teardrops.

Ethereal Aspirations

Bear me aloft,
if only for one day.
I wish to float upon your Zeppelin,
intoxicated, five miles high,

inspired to giddy laughter
at terrestrial mortality.
Perspective is everything
in a world too often ruled

by grey ligatures of terrestrial logic
and imaginations limited by spectral hues.
Liberate your secrets
I will keep them locked within me.

Geese Flying South

The geese
　　　Assume formation
Flying south
　　　What map gives
　　　　　Proper directions?
　　　Who heads the V?
　　　　　Is danger ever
　　　　　　　A passing fearful heartbeat
　　　　　Among the clouds?
　　　　　　　All that rises
　　　　　　　　　One day must descend.
　　　　　　　Who chooses?
　　　　　　　　In the sky
　　　　　　　　　　Does humble Faith exist
　　　　　　　　Does God?
　　　　　I watch you
　　　　　　　Do you feel my prying eyes
　　　　　Upon you?
　　　Do not leave.
　　　　　Questions remain
　　　Unanswered.
　　Would that I
　　　Could join your flock
　　Free in flight.
From behind the trees
　　　A gunshot echoes,

　　A cry,
　　　　formation scatters.

Chanteuse

She has a teardrop voice,
sticky like August dusk.
Leaving syrupy remnants,
it washes my outer layers.

Invisible, her touch, it grasps me from afar,
like a small child begging
with dark imploring eyes
requesting one last candy, please.

At the song's last coda,
her vibrato breaks, the melody is over.
In the background, over the cicadas' chirp,
molasses echoes linger in my ears.

A Bullet's Tale

Marketing dictates morphology
that makes it look like lipstick:
sleek as a cheetah
luxurious and glossy
but seconds later
scarlet spreads
in a jagged circle
that leaves a stain
much harder to erase
than indelible first kiss.

The Dispersal

Some say father is destined
for a better place.

They say their prayers and incantations
but what is better

about this lack of breath,
this silencing

of capsicum thought, chamomile voice?
What is to be desired

in endless time and distance?
I store collected recollections

in my vault
but they won't replace

tamarind wisdom in leathery flesh.
Every sense tells me a different truth.

Internal whispers ask,
who were post-mortem myths invented for?

All I can accept
is that we scattered ashes,

a pale carbon residue
of life well-lived

now washed away
by muddy ebbing waters.

Under My Skin

Your barbs once placed
under my thin epidermal surface,
the hue of lightly roasted coffee,

persist in place despite best efforts
to insulate the present from all past offenses.
Prickling formication reminds

of taunting smiles and ridicule and spit
sent hurtling through hallways
and promises of closed space between us.

Time sharpened some of memory's
grapnels, dulling sundry others
and though I pretend history remains

forgotten and forgiven, though I
lacquer my countenance,
craft a face of smiling dissimulation,

you will always be there
a noxious layer
piercing inside out.

Life Ends in Immolation

Just a footnote in Monday morning's paper
I recognize the picture
from grocery store encounters.
Eyes draw haunting posthumous association.

Why would you choose
to end it all that way
licked and swallowed
by flames' relentless tongues?

When did hope surrender?
The question calls for speculation.
No clues remain, not even a fingerprint.
Flesh burns too quickly, truth is silent bone and ash.

The newsprint says
you gave up hope
when they took your newborn from you,
In my eyes, I see her stubby arms outstretched.

I, but a stranger
bear icy guilt and grief
for soft indifference
that now turns to briar thorn.

The empty swing set creaks,
chain links glistening,
seats blowing in the wind.
None comes to push it.

Painted Lady

Down the dusty road I ramble.
She dips and dances,
swirling overhead

I envy her agility,
wish to possess it.
I reach up—

She eludes my grasp,
then swoops in closer
feigning a kiss.

Beyond arm's length
she teases earthbound feet.
Who is this Painted Lady-

Coquette or gypsy?
Either way my eyes
remind me I am charmed,

blessed to make airborne acquaintance,
short lived but well-remembered,
a flitting wing beat.

In the ICU

After Ezra Pound's "Chi E Questa [Who Is She?]"

Would she have me kneel before her, bend
backward, contort myself to prove my honor?
I, paternal troubadour, sing songs, plant kisses upon her,
seeking nothing more than a nightmare's end.

In the beginning, there is no conception of an end
for the child may just as well be proof, of divinity,
of all potential bounty that exists to be
cultivated, ripened, fed by a robust heart.

But at the last, there is nothing more than grace
No explanation for the girl's departure, wrought
by rogue vascular weakness without a name,
that brought us to this sterile, urgent place
where monitors beep without a thought,
unarticulated love grows weeds of shame.

Before You Walk Away

Before you walk away
across the distant fields, turn back.
Run to me, leap into my arms.

The appointed time is not yet here
I can't allow its imminent arrival
for darkness is not yet fallen.
Let us link fingers until then:

one more smile, sparks igniting,
reflected in turquoise oval eye-pools,
images of tiny narrow feet
that used to skip and dance.

How shall I forestall the ending of this story?
I fall upon the earth. The ferryman has come to carry you.
He has no words. He begs no pardon.

Mukund Gnanadesikan was born in 1970 in Summit, New Jersey, the younger son of two Indian immigrant mathematicians. His life-long struggles with epilepsy and depression imbued him with sympathy for life's underdogs.

He wrote his first poem at age 14, at the suggestion of his English teacher. Twenty years later, this poem was published in the anthology, *Sheets: For Men Only*. His writing journey detoured into sports journalism during his collegiate years, and he did not return to poetry for another decade but has composed intermittently since then.

Gnanadesikan's poetry draws on diverse influences, from the philosophical observations of Rumi to the heart-felt pathos of Tagore and the raw honesty of Jericho Brown. He aims to let readers see themselves in his work while also seeing others, to bridge the divide that is too often felt in our modern, disconnected universe.

www.ingramcontent.com/pod-product-compliance
Lightning Source LLC
Chambersburg PA
CBHW022053080426
42734CB00009B/1322